Finding Rest
in the
Wilderness

By

Robert Benjamin Bamburg

This book is dedicated to my beautiful, patient, understanding wife, Michelle. Thank you for putting up with me while I was trying to figure all this out.

CONTENTS

PREFACE

Many Christians, especially now, feel as though they are in a dry spell. They long for a deeper relationship with God, but can't seem to find the time. I've heard people tell me, "If I could just get a break from the everyday and recharge my batteries..." That will never happen. We have to make time for God in our day to day activities. I remember back when I went to youth camp and asked one of my friends, "How do we take this experience back home?" Because once camp ended life returned to normal. You can't just have a temporary revival, retreat, or camp experience. "Life" will always be there when you get back.

Job had "life" happen to him and he could have responded two different ways. Satan expected Job to fall away and curse God. God expected Job to praise him regardless. We go through the same test. This book was written to show you how to rest when everything is going wrong, how to hold on to the promises of God, how to grow deeper in your relationship instead of giving up hope.

I hadn't had my faith tested until I married my wife. I knew things would be difficult with her in a wheelchair, but there were many more surprises in store for me. I ended up, shortly after eloping in secret, unemployed and living with my mother-n-law newly separated from her husband, my autistic sister-in- law, a family friend, an adopted sister-in-law who had just went through rehab, her teenage friend, a caretaker, and everyone needed something from me. I had to give rides to school or work, loan money, babysit, and, of course, take care of my pregnant wife (which happened three months into our marriage in case you were wondering)). At one point my wife was 6 months pregnant and we were homeless moving from house to hotel to house (friends' or relatives'). Then when I moved back, her adopted sister had an out of wedlock pregnancy and I was the babysitter for her daughter, my sister-in-law and watching my own child. Many thought my wife would need a C-section because of her condition and she birthed Elijah naturally within 15 minutes of her water breaking. No complications. I was unable to make my car payments and God provided through a church money for the 3 past-due payments and kept my car from being repossessed. God showed Himself faithful always providing our needs and keeping us healthy in every situation.

He remains faithful even when we are faithless. We must keep the faith and learn to rest in knowing God. When we seek to know Him, He is happy to show us his goodness and mercy.

CHAPTER 1

THE WILDERNESS

So, as the Holy Spirit says: "Today, if you hear his voice, do not harden your hearts as you did in the rebellion, during the time of testing in the wilderness, where your ancestors tested and tried me, though for forty years they saw what I did. That is why I was angry with that generation; I said, 'Their hearts are always going astray, and they have not known my ways.' So I declared on oath in my anger, 'They shall never enter my rest.' " See to it, brothers and sisters, that none of you has a sinful, unbelieving heart that turns away from the living God. But encourage one another daily, as long as it is called "Today," so that none of you may be hardened by sin's deceitfulness. We have come to share in Christ, if indeed we hold firmly till the end our original conviction. As has just been said: *"Today, if you hear his voice, do not harden your hearts as you did in the rebellion." - Hebrews 3:7-15 (TNIV)*

How can anyone find rest in the wilderness? No one makes their home in the wilderness. Unless you belong to the Swiss Family Robinson. We want to build houses, shelter, civilization and nest. We want control over our environment; not become vulnerable. If we didn't have a home to store all our things in, then everything could get stolen or damaged. If we didn't have a job, then we couldn't provide for our families. We need insurance on our cars, our homes, even our lives for security. That's why the wilderness scares us.

However, back in the days of Adam and Eve there was no man-made security. They didn't need clothes or shelter. No rain or precipitation, why have a roof? If you eat straight from a tree there is no need for a fridge or oven. Before the curse, no thorns grew in the ground, so soft grass would make a nice bed. Adam and Eve walked with God in the cool of the day in their wilderness. Perhaps God is trying to call us back to that paradise; to have communion with him in the midst of our "wilderness" experience and learn dependence on Him. Did not Abraham, the Israelites, and even Jesus wander the desert?

They all had their trust in God tested and afterward received a blessing, inheritance or promise. At the same time, they learned of and physically saw God's faithfulness and provision. He provided Abraham a sacrifice to replace Isaac, the Israelites food and water in the desert, Jesus had the Holy Spirit to sustain him while he laid down his deity. You may feel as though you have walked in circles never getting closer to your promise. The good news is that you have already received the promise if you have received Jesus as your Savior. However, you must walk in it to experience it. Walking in the promise allows us to see who God is: Our provider, our peace, our healer, our banner, our righteousness, our everything.

But how do you walk in the promise and disregard all the circumstances you are in? What does it take to get to that place of rest Hebrews speaks of? What IS the promise?

He redeemed us in order that the blessing given to Abraham might come to the Gentiles through Christ Jesus, so that by faith we might receive the promise of the Spirit. - Galatians 3:14 (TNIV)

CHAPTER 2
IT'S ABOUT CHARACTER

In order to get through the wilderness we need to be mindful of the reason we are traveling. It is to build character, to show God's character to others, and to grow intimate with God. We must keep the mentality that everything is for his glory. Even for the seasoned Christian, things arise and we still forget why. I had been one for seventeen years, grown up in church, yet I didn't see how God used me during the toughest of times. In my trials He showed those around me his goodness and his character. He showed people through me his strength to press through a difficult situation. He kept me from cursing, fighting, becoming bitter. Whatever weakness I had or showed lasted only for a moment. I didn't live in bitterness. Instead, those around me saw the love I had for my wife and taking care of her while in a wheelchair and pregnant, as well as taking care of her family and friends. They could tell I was tired, but saw God's faithfulness in me (2 Corinthians 4:7). God sustained me and strengthened me. We need to serve as lights to the world. We need to reflect God so they can see the hope that lies within (2 Corinthians 3:18). We show God's character when we allow the Holy

Spirit to control our lives.

Joseph had a destiny. God wanted to bring him to prosperity beyond what he had. He began as the favored son of his father, and then seemingly downgraded to a slave, then a prisoner. He, however, knew God's character. He had no doubt heard of his family's legacy. His great-grandfather being led by faith to a great land and God giving him a son at 100 years of age. Then how his grandfather nearly died at the hands of his father, but an angel saved his life. His father's vision of heaven. He himself was a miracle because of his mother's bareness, and yet he is born of her through God's favor and the prayer of his parents. He had a legacy of devotion to God and miracles happening. He realized that God favored him as well and never lost sight of God's goodness. God gave him favor with his master and everything Joseph touched prospered. Potiphar's wife saw Joseph's devotion when he refused to sleep with her. Joseph also proved himself as a man of character to the prison guard. Joseph used his God-given gift of wisdom while in prison and did not spite God. When he has the chance to get even with his brothers and curse them to their face for putting him through all these things he doesn't. Listen to what he says instead. *"You intended to harm me, but God intended it for good to accomplish what is now being done, the saving of many lives. " -Genesis 50:20 (TNIV).* Joseph knew God, not his brothers, was in charge of his destiny. He basically thanked his brothers for selling him and then gave them honor by inviting them to feast at the palace.

When going through the wilderness we have a

chance to minister to others around us. They may see the difficult times we go through and begin to understand who God is through your trust in him. They can see God's character manifested in you.

This doesn't mean you have to ignore the problem. It is okay to see the problem. If we didn't notice a problem we wouldn't go to God for the solution. It is okay to pour out your complaint, but never curse, defame or deny God's character (Psalm 142:2).

Job was overwhelmed with problems. God allowed Satan to torture this man in every way. He killed his children, stole his wealth, plagued him with disease. He just left him terrible friends and a nagging wife. However, Job defended the character of God. He praised him for his wealth, because he knew by himself he could do nothing. He understood that God had his hand on him keeping him from disaster up until now. He did complain about his situation, but he never defamed God. In the end God defended Job and found fault with his self- righteous friends. Job offered a sacrifice for them for God's forgiveness. Like Joseph, he showed grace and kindness to those who hurt him.

We need to recognize the grace of God in our situation and show it to others. It serves as a witness to others, and at the same time, strengthens us when we are weak. His grace is sufficient in our weaknesses (2 Corinthians 12:9). Look at the past to get through the tough times. David looked back and said *"You have done many good things for me, LORD, just as you promised." -Psalm 119:65 (NLT)* and then said *"My eyes are straining to see your promises come true. When will you comfort me? " -Psalm 119:82 (NLT)* He remembered God's goodness and expected history to repeat itself. He did stress at times, but he stayed in the Spirit and wrote the Psalms praising God for his works and for his character. He recounted works as far back as the plagues on Egypt and parting the Red Sea. He praised Him for his heritage. We must do the same and rejoice with other Christians when God blesses them and expect the same great things for ourselves for God is not a respecter of persons. We are all descendants of Abraham. He will show you the same goodness.

CHAPTER 3
DISTRACTION OR MOTIVATION?

I've heard from many people that they want to grow closer to God, but need a break from the everyday life in order to focus on him. That will never happen, because God needs to be a part of your everyday life. No matter how busy your day is, if God comes first on your priority list, you will have time for him.

You need to understand that all these distractions should serve as your motivation. They cause awareness of your need for God, but instead you have labeled them distractions by thinking you need to take care of them. The Bible says to cast your cares upon the Lord, because he cares for you and he will sustain you (Psalm 55:22, 1 Peter 5:7). It's a Martha/Mary situation.

Martha wanted to be with Jesus, but had to take care of the household chores before she would listen to him. Mary, on the other hand, saw him there and came to him as soon as he showed up. Martha rebuked Mary and told Jesus to make her help, but he scolded her and said Mary has found the one thing that truly matters and he would not take it from her (Luke 10:38-42). We've heard that story many times before, but I doubt many understood the significance of that story in their own lives.

I have to ask, if you already feel ill-equipped for the day and your stress levels rising, why wait until you have completed the impossible to seek God? These responsibilities have become idols in your life. You serve them before God and allow them to keep you from God. God has a rather difficult time getting our attention. He will give blessings to show us he cares, and we'll focus on the gifts instead of the giver. Or he'll give us troubles to seek Him, and we focus on the problems instead of the solution.

When Goliath came to terrorize Israel's camp, Saul offered David armor and a sword. David knew he didn't need weapons or great strength. Everyone who depended on their own strength hid and avoided Goliath. David depended upon God and slew Goliath with little muscle using only a stone and a slingshot. David saw Goliath as another chance for God to show his goodness before Israel and their enemies, not as an obstacle. He told others, "God delivered a lion and bear to me, if you don't believe me watch me take care of this giant" (1 Samuel 17:36). We need to see that God is more than enough in every situation.

Jesus said apart from him we could do nothing (John 15:5). Proverbs says unless the Lord builds a house, they labor in vain who build it (Psalm 127:1). Proverbs also says to commit your work to the Lord and he will make your plans succeed (Proverbs 6:13).

God will give you his strength, his wisdom, his provision, his ability to take care of your needs. So let the baby cry for a couple minutes, take a minute to pray when running late for work to give God just a moment of undivided attention. I found out early on God can take care of time. I'd hit every red light, but God gave me favor with my boss and co-workers. Jesus said to seek first the kingdom and his righteousness and then everything will be added to you (Matthew 6:33).

CHAPTER 4
JUST WAIT

My favorite question is "when?". That word accounts for half of my prayer life. "When will I receive healing?" "When will I receive financial security/independence?" "When will I receive what you promised?" Unfortunately, I have to tell you the "when" is probably after your bills are outstanding, maybe even after your utilities are shut off, or fifteen minutes after you should have shown up for work. "When" as far as you are concerned, will probably be too late. However, God will show you more of his glory if you choose to wait after your designated deadline.

"Jesus, my brother has fallen ill and on his deathbed. You must come quick to heal him!" Martha exclaimed. Jesus sent her word that the sickness would not end in death and waited several days after the man had already died to show up. Martha confronts Jesus, rather aggravated, and informs him that if he had been there sooner Lazarus would not have died. He reminds her that he told her she would see God's glory. He asks those around where they put Lazarus, and they tell him they placed him in a tomb.

Then Jesus weeps. Ironically, not after the people tell him Lazarus died, but after they tell him they buried him. He cried because of their lack of belief. He uses Lazarus' death to show people it is never too late for God to intervene. Jesus raises Lazarus from the dead, not after just a moment, or just a day, but SEVERAL days! (John 11:1-44)

God is not a sadist. He doesn't torture you for fun. However, it may feel like He puts you on the rack when you stretch out of your comfort zone and have to use the faith granted you. When you take matters into your own hands and assume you are more responsible then God you fall into trouble. Don't take out a loan, don't use the credit card, don't go outside the provision God gave you to pay for anything. You will lose more than what you wanted to attain.

Solomon instructed Saul to wait a number of days for him to return before trying to inquire of God or go to battle. Saul waits until the last minute and then takes the situation into his own hands and makes his own sacrifice to please faithless people rather than God. He essentially pushes the man of God aside and forsakes his instructions, promotes himself to a priest or prophet's status and then, because of his disobedience, God takes his entire kingdom away and gives it to David (1 Samuel 13:8-14). The chapter before Samuel tells the people, "Even when you sin against God, don't think he has abandoned you and do not look to anything other than Him, because it will not profit or rescue you at all" (1 Samuel 12:20,21).

Jesus waited until Lazarus died before he came to

heal him to show everyone that, for him, even grave circumstances are not that urgent. Things that seem irreversible are not so. In that act Jesus proves he will carry out his word even when hope seems lost. He has overcome the world and the grave (John 16:33, Revelation 1:18). What more shall we fear? Jesus asks the question *"Is not life more important than food, and the body more important than clothes?" (Matthew 6:25 TNIV)* So do not worry about anything except seeking his kingdom and his righteousness (Matthew 6:33).

In actuality, God doesn't look at time, he looks more at circumstance. He looks at someone's heart. Trying to prove to them where they are at spiritually. He does not test us to see where we stand. He tests us for us to see where we stand. Do we truly trust and depend on God like we say we do? Do we honestly think we have faith? Faith and anxiety cannot co-exist. We feel anxiety because without him we are weak. In Isaiah though, the prophet informs us God does not grow weary nor tired. If we wait on the Lord, we will receive his strength and transform into his likeness. We will not grow weary or tired either (Isaiah 40:28-31).

If you are stuck in traffic, usually it causes stress to rise. Why? Because people have an agenda and the stalled cars are keeping them from it. You need to get something done. However, if we wait on God that should not cause stress, because he is taking care of it. Are you worried about work? God is Jehovah Jireh, your provider (Genesis 22:14). Are you worried about healing? God is Jehovah Rapha, your healer (Exodus 15:26). Are you worried about an addiction? God is your Jehovah Nissi, your victor (Exodus 17:15). Are you worried in general? God is Jehovah Shalom, your peace (Judges 6:24). Are you worried your sin separated you from God? God is Jehovah Shammah/ M'kaddesh/Tsidkenu, He is there, sanctifies, and serves as your righteousness (Ezekiel 48:35, Exodus 31:13, Jeremiah 23:6) Just wait for Him to answer.

CHAPTER 5
LEARNING DEPENDENCE

As I pointed out in the last chapter, we often act out of self- sufficiency, especially if God takes too long to answer. Or, if we can't do it on our own, we look to our worldly network of friends: Visa, Discover, movies, television, doctors, etc. Instead we have to recognize our need for God. Develop a dependence on God (Psalm 127:1, John 15:5).

God shows his abundance in the wilderness: a great river springing forth from a rock in the desert (Exodus 17:1-7), a jar of oil never running dry for seven years (1 Kings 17:12-16), bread and fish multiplying enough to feed crowds of 5,000 and 4,000 (Matthew 16:9,10). Until we rid ourselves of every other source we cannot fully grasp the greatness of God. When living in a place of lack we need not gripe at God and find something better, we instead need to speak truth about the situation. God will supply all your needs according to his riches and glory (Philippians 4:19).

Too many times we look at God's promises as empty words instead of cherishing and hoping in them like silver or gold. We want control and the ability to manipulate circumstances like little children instead of just asking the authority figure. God is the one source that does not manipulate or take advantage of you. When will we realize these other sources actually steal everything from us? "How many organs need to be taken out and how many more side effects do I have to suffer before I am healed or at least feeling better?" "How much debt and stress do I have to endure before I can really own anything?" "I thought I could have it all and now the repo men are taking it all!" There are only two sources: the God of Heaven, or the god of this world, Satan. Remember what Samuel said in 1 Samuel 12:20,21? It is vanity to trust in anything else.

TV has become the worst tool in our arsenal for taking care of things. We use it to babysit the kids, to entertain the teenagers, to unwind after a hard day of work. For infants, TV hinders brain development. For children, it affects their attention span. For teens, it demoralizes them and strips them of all the values their parents tried to instill in them. For men, it distracts from their relationship with their families. For women, it can make them question their own marriage and family. This is all of course generally speaking, but mainstream TV does teach self-indulgence, greed, disrespect and mainstreams everything Paul said people would become in the last days. (Yes, I intentionally used that word twice.)

"But mark this: There will be terrible times in the last days. People will be lovers of themselves, lovers of money, boastful, proud, abusive, disobedient to their parents, ungrateful, unholy,

without love, unforgiving, slanderous, without self-control, brutal, not lovers of the good, treacherous, rash, conceited, lovers of pleasure rather than lovers of God-- having a form of godliness but denying its power. Have nothing to do with such people. They are the kind who worm their way into homes and gain control over gullible women, who are loaded down with sins and are swayed by all kinds of evil desires, always learning but never able to come to a knowledge of the truth " - 2 Timothy 3:1-7 (TNIV)

Depending on God also means becoming interdependent with the church. The church functions as Christ's body so it serves as one of his provisions (1 Corinthians 12:25-27). We need God and we need his people to fellowship and become family. Even since the beginning God recognized it was not good for a man to be alone (Genesis 2:18). According to the second chapter of Acts the church met daily in each others houses breaking bread, and reading the Word and having everything in common. They united to build up one another. I believe that is part of the reason they performed so many miracles back then (Acts 2:42-47). Do you know that God looked at a rebellious people that united together in one cause to build the tower of Babel and said nothing would be impossible for them because of their unity (Genesis 11:1-9)? How much more righteous children of God? In contrast, a house divided against itself cannot stand (Luke 11:17).

Everyone thinks of Elijah as superhuman because of the miracles he did. We believe it would take a great amount of faith for us to do those same things.

However, James stresses that Elijah was just like the rest of us (James 5:17). Elijah acted fickle just like we do. You think he had great faith all the time? Not at all. After God sent fire down from heaven to consume the sacrifice and allowed Elijah to kill all those servants of Baal, he ran for his life from just one woman. He felt like dying because of her threats (1 Kings 19:1-4). God realizes our small frame and frail minds. That's why He gave you everything pertaining to life and godliness through his Word and makes sure to tell you study daily (2 Peter 1:3). Crucify the flesh daily, encourage one another daily and do not forsake assembling yourselves together (Hebrews 3:13, 10:25). We need the church and the church needs us. Not just for Sundays, but for encouragement, building faith and seeing God manifest his presence when we praise him. More of God comes when two or more are gathered in his name (Matthew 18:19,20). We need to recognize that whatever weakness we have God can use and strengthen (2 Corinthians 12:10). God can even increase our faith when we feel too weak. If Jesus said that the world's sin was unbelief in him (John 16:9) and in Romans it says where sin abounds grace much more abounds (Romans 5:20), God can cover our lack of faith (Mark 9:24). Even the faith to receive salvation did not originate from ourselves but God (Ephesians 2:8). We need to recognize our dependence on Him, and realize He is the answer to everything. God is more than enough for every situation and every weakness.

CHAPTER 6
ENTERING THAT REST

When the Israelites complained in the desert God vowed that they would never enter his "rest". I want you to understand that statement. They refused to mature and God could not give them their promise in that state. If you have a fragile valuable heirloom you want to pass down to your children, when would you give it to them? When they could handle the item with appreciation and with great care. If I try to give nearly anything to my toddler when he is angry, he will throw it to the ground, even if it was the very thing he wanted but I took too long in giving it to him. The "rest" referred to the Promised Land.

Hebrews tells of a greater "rest" for Christians. The rest is the promised Holy Spirit. Jesus promised his disciples that they would receive the Holy Spirit, the comforter and counselor. The Holy Spirit gives us access to Heaven (Matthew 16:19). He serves as a seal for those who belong to Christ (2 Corinthians 1:22). Hebrews tells us to labor to enter that rest daily, and not to harden our hearts as the Israelites did in their rebellion (Hebrews 3:7-19).

"And you also were included in Christ when you heard the word of truth, the gospel of your salvation. When you believed, you were marked in him with a seal, the promised Holy Spirit," - Ephesians 1:13 (TNIV)

When a person receives Jesus as their savior, they receive the Holy Spirit at that moment. From then on he needs to mature and develop the ability to live in the Spirit. This is what Paul is referring to. We need to lay down everything that gets in the way of serving God and hardens our heart against him: our pride, our own desires, our sins, our insecurities, everything. Jesus calls to all those heavy laden to take his yoke upon them and they will find rest for their souls (Matthew 11:28-30). A yoke joins two oxen to share the labor and keep them going the same direction. The Holy Spirit joins us with Christ and helps us carry our load.

The choice comes daily. Whether you want to join with God or go on your own. When we do not join with Him our hearts will become hardened against him. God cannot give anything to a hardened heart. It deadens our senses (Matthew 13:14,15). We cannot see Him working in our lives, we cannot hear Him speak to us, or understand what is going on around us. Jesus says these things specifically in the Gospels. Even if God did work a miracle for you, you could not perceive it with your heart hardened against him (Luke 16:31).

Joining or uniting with God is where we find the answer to everything. Jesus said if we abode in him and his words in us we would receive whatever we ask for in prayer (John 15:7). Jesus prayed in John chapter 17 that we would be in him just as he is in the Father. The reason we find rest in him is because we have faith in him. I don't mean we just trust him. We trust him because we are in him.

Would anyone doubt that God would not answer a prayer from Jesus? But we often feel like our prayers don't make it past the ceiling. We have the authority to use Jesus' name in prayers, casting out demons, and casting off sickness just as he did (Matthew 10:1). We have the ability to hear God's voice (John 10:1-6), the ability to overcome the enemy (Luke 10:19), the ability to be heard by God (Isaiah 59:1). Looking at the scriptures, when we receive salvation we are no longer the same person, we are in Christ (2 Corinthians 5:17). So many people strive until they get to Heaven before they find rest, but they don't understand they already have it. Jesus says in that same prayer that those that believe the gospel are no longer of the world but of Heaven (John 17:16). He told his disciples that whatever we bind on earth will be bound in Heaven and whatever we loose on earth will be loosed in Heaven (Matthew 16:19).

In order to have the rest and peace we are looking for, we must be in tune with God's Spirit by praying and reading the scriptures. We don't know what we have unless we read his Word.

CHAPTER 7
UNDERSTANDING FAITH

Exercising faith, though it may seem complicated, is as easy as just speaking God's Word.

"Now faith is the substance of things hoped for, the evidence of things not seen." (Hebrews 11:1 KJV) God's Son and his Word and his Spirit are all connected. In the beginning was the Word and the Word was with God and the Word was God and the Word became flesh, which refers to Jesus, according to John 1. Jesus says his words are spirit (John 6:63). Therefore God's Word tells us of things we cannot see, it is our evidence of what we have, and the Holy Spirit substantiates what we expect to come. In simpler terms. The Bible tells us what we have access to, or a promise for us to stand on. Since the Bible is unchanging truth, we have that as our proof that these things exist and that we have ownership of them. The Holy Spirit makes it happen in the physical.

Another example: creation. God spoke everything into existence. He spoke the word, and the Holy Spirit created the worlds. So when God gives you a promise, you speak that promise being sure of it in your heart, and the Holy Spirit will make that happen (Mark 11:23,24). We are made in the image of God and our words have a similar power (Genesis 1:26). When we pray "in Jesus name" it is not a ritual, but a reminder of where we stand. When we receive salvation we are "in Christ". So when we pray his word, we know it is according to his will and we can have faith that it will happen, because it is just as if he prayed that prayer (1 John 5:14). It's his own words (Isaiah 55:11).

Faith seems so difficult at times, you think it's not that easy to see a miracle just by speaking a word. That is because you are not convinced of what you are speaking. How do you become convinced of something? You look for evidence. The more evidence you have, the more confidence or trust you have. Remember faith is the evidence of things unseen. How do you get the faith? *"Faith cometh by hearing, and hearing by the Word of God" -Romans 10:17 (KJV)* It comes by hearing the Bible. Speak scriptures concerning your prayer request over and over again. There is a connection between your heart and your speech. *"For of the abundance of the heart his mouth speaketh" - Luke 6:45 (KJV) "Let the words of my mouth, and the meditation of my heart, be acceptable in thy sight, O LORD, my strength and my redeemer." - Psalm 19:14 (KJV)* This process of speaking and believing gave us salvation (Romans 10:9).

You may still wonder how to gain certainty if you don't understand scripture. Don't worry. Even if you are unsure of what scripture means we are told in the Bible that the Holy Spirit will teach us how to discern the scriptures (1 John 2:27). James says if we need wisdom just ask God and he will give it (James 1:5).

Looking back at the connection of heart, faith, and scripture. Take a look at three scriptures. Genesis 15:6, Romans 14:23, and Psalms 119:11. Abraham's belief (faith) was considered righteousness. Paul says anything outside of faith is sin. David says he hid God's Word in his heart so that he would not sin. It is impossible to please God without faith or trust (Hebrews 11:6). You can't operate in signs, wonders, miracles, or even just righteousness without knowing God's Word. When we do have the scriptures and they become a part of our daily life we can accomplish anything (John 15:7).

So listen to the Bible on CD in the car, or write scriptures on posters or sticky notes and post them all over the house. Choose verses that apply to what you need so you can trust God to give it to you. The Bible has verses pertaining to strength, patience, money, job, pregnancy, health, nearly anything. To help you in your search, you can look for Bible search engines online and type in key words. This is what's needed the most for you to see change in your life.

CHAPTER 8
HOPE, TODAY

We cannot predict the future or change the future, just the present. This inability keeps us from jumping ahead of God. It also helps us not to focus on the disappointments of yesterday. It keeps us joyful, expectant and excited. If I focus on something other than today, I put myself in God's shoes who is outside time. I don't belong there because I'm not God and I can't control anything outside my domain.

I've had trouble with this area. I would focus on my wife's handicap and not her healing. I became furious when she told me her past experiences and pain. I looked at her today and saw her in a wheelchair, same as yesterday, and expect the same tomorrow. But God said we have a promise of healing, and if I received "the promise" I already have the answer. If God cannot speak a lie and says by Jesus' stripes she is healed, she is healed (Isaiah 53:5). I might not have seen her healed yesterday, but she IS today. That's present tense.

How excited are you the day you get a brand new car, or home, or get accepted to college, or find out you're pregnant? You revel in the moment. However, when you sign the title you usually aren't experiencing what you've gotten. You sign the title in an office and then enjoy your home or your car. You had it before you jumped in and turned the key. You get accepted to a college before you go to college. So my wife has received healing even if she hasn't "experienced" it yet. Why should I be disappointed if she hasn't experienced yet? Shouldn't I have the same joyful and grateful attitude before and after the experience. Reason being, I become depressed focusing on everything she has missed out on and hope she can have better experiences in the future. The very moment she gets up and walks her past still hasn't changed. She still hasn't ice skated or ridden a bike or gone swimming, but she has the ability to do that later. Well doesn't she have the ability to do that "later" now? So I should either be just as depressed the moment she is healed, or just as joyful now as when I see her healed. Which makes more sense? I have hope for the future because I have the promise.

When a student reads an acceptance letter, does he or she become depressed that they aren't already in school? Or do they rejoice in knowing they WILL go?

If we rejoice in a fickle man's promise, shouldn't we be even more excited and all the more joyful in a promise made by an eternal God?

The Bible tells us the things that are whether or not we have experienced them. We hope for physical things because we cannot see them yet, but we experience the spiritual. You have citizenship in Heaven, but for now are on the earth (Ephesians 2:6).

You have everything up there, but need it to come down.

So Jesus gave you the keys to the Kingdom of Heaven to bring your inheritance to the earth. The Holy Spirit delivers your blessings and the fruit of the Spirit sustains you while hoping for them to come. You may see the exact opposite of what you wanted happening. Don't go by your senses or what you experience. Keep the faith. We know whatever bad happens, it's already been taken care of. (Genesis 50:20, Romans 8:28) Remember Lazarus.

One thing I have to stress, because I have not lived it, but just now received this revelation. Be thankful for what you cannot see. I thought I wasn't mature enough to receive something and wondered "What more does God want from me?" Thankfulness. We must be anxious for nothing, but with thanksgiving make our requests known (Philippians 4:6). Thank Him for what you don't see. If you believed you already received, you would act the same way (Mark 11:24). You would be on your face praising God for something so miraculous and at a loss for words rather than finding an abundance of words to tell Him in your anger. Trusting and showing gratitude proves maturity.

CHAPTER 9

FOCUS ON THE SPIRITUAL

The wilderness experience is to get us in tune with the Holy Spirit. We must have an eternal focus. We see ourselves in the natural, often falling into sin, not having enough faith, not having "arrived" in our spiritual walk, while God sees something entirely different. He sees his perfect Son. He sees you as having "arrived" and uses all these trials to get you to see what he sees. You are the righteousness of God in Christ (2 Corinthians 5:21). You have the mind of Christ (1 Corinthians 2:16). You have the fullness of God in you (Ephesians 3:19). Paul realized this and prayed the church would receive revelation of these things in the book of Ephesians.

Maturing as a Christian, just as it is in adulthood, is finding out who you are. Teenagers search for who they are apart from their families. We often encounter it again when becoming an empty-nester or middle-aged. Often because we put our identity in doing something or being with someone. Who am I without kids, without parents, without a spouse, without a job, without...? Paul looked at everything he had as well: I am a Pharisee of Pharisees, from the tribe of

Benjamin... yet he considered his pedigree and prestige as nothing compared to knowing Jesus as his Lord (Philippians 3:3-9)

Why? Anything else you could try to cling to will vanish. God will never leave you nor forsake you (Psalms 94:14). He gives you eternal security. He knew you before you were formed in your mother's womb, and his thoughts about you outnumber the grains of sand (Jeremiah 1:5, Psalms 139:17,18). Therefore we find our identity and our worth in Him.

James tells us listening to the Word and not obeying is like someone looking in a mirror and forgetting what kind of man he is (James 1:23-24). That is because Jesus is the Word, and we are made in his image (Romans 8:29). We must read the Bible and act on it. Be anxious for nothing (Philippians 4:6). Do not stifle the Holy Spirit (1 Thessalonians 5:19). Today if you hear his voice, do not harden your heart (Hebrews 3:15). Remember the parable of the two houses? One was built on sand and the other on rock. The one on the rock stood firm (Matthew 7:24- 25). The rains came to both houses, building on the rock didn't keep a storm from coming, but it kept the house stable and secure.

The daily renewing of our minds through scripture serves as our stability. These desert times come much more than once in a lifetime. Look at Paul's laundry list of trials: being stoned, shipwrecked, imprisoned, lost at sea, flogged, whipped, going hungry and naked (2 Corinthians 11:23-27). Passing the test in the wilderness does not keep you from trials later on, but it does show you how to overcome them: by relying on Jesus' strength (Psalm 34:19).

During trials, especially regarding relationships, we must call things that are not as though they were. If you have a verbally abusive, or distant husband, do not treat him as one. See that Jesus took his sins, and picture him as the perfect man you wanted. Lavish love on him as though he were perfect. If you have a nagging, manipulative wife, do the same thing. If you have a wayward son or daughter, love them through whatever hurt they cause you. Picture perfection. See things as though God accomplished his work, and live in it (Romans 4:17-24). This builds your faith and keeps you from the hurt. Know that one day it will manifest. God can turn the heart of a leader like the course of the river, he can harden and soften hearts (Proverbs 21:1, Ezekiel 36:26). When something requires an "act of God", realize that is not far off. A miracle from God is very much available to you.

In Eden, Adam and Eve had experienced perfection. They walked with God in the cool of the day and were without insecurity. Once they questioned God's word and disobeyed by eating the forbidden fruit, they lost it all. Jesus came as the second Adam to restore all things (Romans 5:11-21). He reconciled us with God through his death on the cross. Now when we walk by the Spirit we enter Paradise once again, taking him at his Word. Satan cannot steal a thing from you, but will try to deceive you and take your hope. We stand against him with the shield of faith by trusting in the Bible. Then we realize the curse no longer applies to us (Galatians 3:13). We may be in a desert, but God said he would make the wastelands bountiful (Isaiah 35). Our inheritance causes things around us to change. We are no longer of this world, but citizens of Heaven thus whatever we loose on earth will be loosed in heaven (Matthew 16:19).

If you have received Christ, you have died (Galatians 2:20). When someone dies they are buried in the ground and the tombstone reads what? RIP. When we die to ourselves and to sin we will rest in peace. The Bible says to pick up our cross, or crucify ourselves daily (Luke 9:23). Daily surrender everything. You should not have a mind of your own, otherwise it would fight the mind of Christ (Romans 8:7). Do not just lay down your weaknesses before God. Lay down your strengths as well. Lay down your all. Realize that the promises and the power rest in his hands and not yours (Psalms 127:1). You can do nothing a part from God (John 15). We must stop looking at our preconceived ideas of how things should happen, and why we don't see what we desire here on earth. Instead we must look to Heaven, not as a future destination, but as a present reality. That is our resting place.

"Therefore we do not lose heart. Though outwardly we are wasting away, yet inwardly we are being renewed day by day. For our light and momentary troubles are achieving for us an eternal glory that far outweighs them all. So we fix our eyes not on what is seen, but on what is unseen, since what is seen is temporary, but what is unseen is eternal. ." - 2 Corinthians 4:16- 18 (TNIV)

ABOUT THE AUTHOR

Basically I'm just an average person with some cool ideas. Nothing really praise-worthy. No degree, no accolades. I have a wife and kids. (We had another son since this book came out.)

I try to keep a blog. Sometimes I don't write in it as much because I'm focusing on writing another book, but there are a number of good articles at www.rbbamburg.com And then in addition to that I have a ministry YouTube channel RBBamburg and a personal one called VloggerTroubles if you're curious what my life is like. Forewarning though, just about everything I do is sporadic.

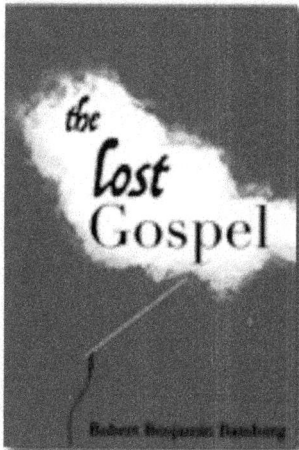

www.ingramcontent.com/pod-product-compliance
Lightning Source LLC
Chambersburg PA
CBHW071243090426
42736CB00014B/3197